One Hundred Poems

One Hundred Poems
Two worlds from my perspective

By Peter Jackson

Spiritual Truth Publishing

Spiritual Truth Publishing
87 Higher Parr Street
St Helens
WA9 1AD
www.spiritualtruth.co.uk

ISBN: 978-0-9931423-0-7

Cover design by Peter Jackson

Set in 13/15 Book Antiqua
Typesetting by
MorganStudios, Cockermouth, Cumbria

Printed and bound by
Printdomain, Thurnscoe, Rotherham, South Yorkshire

For Mam

Contents

Waking up

When you awake after a long peaceful night,
you open your eyes to today's new delight,
say hello to the world and greet with a smile
whatever you do - and do it with style.

Get out of bed, cleanse with a shower,
see it as light, just giving you power.
Go down the stairs, have a nice brew,
maybe some breakfast, then look out at the dew,

that lovely fresh grass grown through the night
looking as earthly as it glistens in light.
The sun may be out, or maybe a cloud -
do not despair, it's a heavenly shroud.

Off you go to your job or to the gym,
to balance your life, keep yourself slim,
clearing your mind and helping your heart,
your body and spirit doing their part.
We know we don't live in that ideal place
but the thought, I do hope, has put a smile on your face.

What if we changed

What if we changed the way that we see?
If I became you and you became me,
what could we change and what could we mend,
what kind of message do you think I would send?
If you saw the world through my innocent eyes
would you regret all the anger and lies?
I'm not judging nor casting you out,
nor am I angry – I don't know how to shout.

You see, I'm a child that has not yet reached birth
and I know nothing about the state of the earth.
I'm sure I'm about to taste that fresh air
and just want to know how safe it is there.
You see, I'm a spirit that waits to be born
but don't want to get there if the earth is war torn.
So, Mr President, please take a step back –
do you think when I come out, I'll want to rush back?
The first thing I see will change all my life
so let it be beauty not trouble and strife.

Where has all the passion gone?

Where has all the passion gone,
the passion for what you do,
the plan you had to change your life,
to show the world you're you?

You know the one; it's in your mind,
it used to be your heart.
And now the dreams and hopes you had,
decided they must part.
But just remember they're still there;
it's just that they are lost.
Find them quickly while you can,
no matter what the cost.

Don't go through life wishing you had done it years ago.
Don't give up just because you fail – have another go.
Don't let yourself be judged by folk,
when they don't even care.
Tell the world you have a dream.
and make it known you're there.

Where can we go?

Where can a lion walk with a deer
and there is no killer instinct
and no natural fear?
Where can the sun shine on the snow
yet not melt it, just make it glow?
Where can man fight, but only use talk
and walk safely on the streets of New York?
Where is this world that all this could be?
Surely not where I live, or can I not see?

The spirit within us can see it around,
but never quite reach it because we are bound
to learn all our lessons on this physical plane,
to walk through the snow and the wind and the rain.
But once our long journey is near an end
our friends in the spirit world, those who transcend,
will take us to heaven – to that place we have seen,
that does all the above, just like it was in our dreams.
And when we are there, what can we do?
Can we look at our lives and think it all through?
Can we change what we were and what we have done?
Or can we atone and simply move on?
The secret is simple, for now we have shed
that physical body and put it to bed.
We don't know all the answers but advice we can give,
with an unbiased opinion to help you to live.
In a world where time plays no part in our task,
we are only a thought away, so the question you ask
is what is it like in this world that you tour?
Well it's just like our old one,
but with all love and no war.

The visiting angel

This is for the angel, who visited last night,
the one that stood before me
beautiful and bright.
You came to help me with my life
and to let me know you're near.
I've been crying as my loved one's gone,
and now things are so clear.

I've done a lot of thinking,
and now I have this thought:
it is your guidance and your help
that I have always sought.
I know I didn't realise it,
but now I know my path.
Thanks for coming here last night,
we did have such a laugh!

Facebook

Facebook and the drama,
showing all our life,
talking about our estranged hubby,
or how we love our wife.
Just had dinner, got a beer,
tell you what I did last year.

Read a status, put a like,
tell some friends to take a hike.
Delete and block so they don't look
at your life that's like a book.
It's not all bad though, there's the thing;
there are some praises we can sing.

You meet new families, read their lives,
and even meet your future wives.
Just think on when feeling low,
Facebook's not the place to go.

Put a coat on, take a walk,
find a friend so that you can talk.
Sit and chat to your hubby or wife,
don't let Facebook be your life.
It's good sometimes when you are bored,
your family's around but you're being ignored,
to jump on Facebook, write a blog,
and tell that you've been to the bog.

Yes some comments make me smile
and some make me run a mile.
I like statuses that are true,
but please don't tell me
when you've been for a poo!

The angel

Who are you? I said to the light,
the one that woke me in the middle of the night.
Why are you here? as I covered my head.
Are you an angel? Am I really dead?

Why do you shine so bright in my eyes?
Am I really frightened or is it surprise?
Why don't you speak?
Let me hear your voice,
I command you now stranger;
that is my choice.

As I plucked up the courage to open my eyes,
I realised there's no fear, so it must be surprise.
Standing before me was an angel in light,
there to protect me whilst I slept through the night.

Still smiling down, as I took a deep breath,
this is my guardian, not a bringer of death.
Thank you for caring and please share my love,
for now I believe in that heaven above.

In the spirit world

In the spirit world – that higher plane –
is where we ascend when we let go of that pain.
That time that we pass from this place we call life,
the moment we leave our husband or wife

It's not unlike the life on this earth,
it's a bit like dying and having rebirth.
Instead of all wars and violence and hate,
we walk to our garden through that heavenly gate.
We don't see God sitting on his throne
and neither and never are we alone.
Here are our loved ones that help with transition,
loving and caring and instant recognition.

Even though they'd gone years before,
that familiar face when you walk through the door.
For now is the time for your body to rest
and your spirit to look at what it could have done best.
Who did we help? Who did we hurt?
What disasters can we now help to avert?

Who do we visit? What do we say?
We go to a medium just to say:
tell 'em I'm fine and my spirit lives on,
tell 'em to imagine me – that I've never gone.
Tell 'em this world is just like before,
but now it's so beautiful with all love and no war.

Heaven

What is in heaven – is it just in our head?
What will happen to us when our bodies are dead?
Do we exist on a spiritual plane?
Is there reincarnation – are we born again?

What is in heaven – what's waiting for us
when we leave this earth, when we get off this bus?
Is it all love or is that just what they say?
How can it be true – is it so far away?

What is in heaven – will I see my dad?
He was in my dream last night and he looked sad.
Was that a reflection of how I am feeling?
Or isn't dad happy – is that what I'm revealing?

What is in heaven – what will I find?
I suppose I'm not dead yet, so I'll make up my mind.
You have to believe that there's something out there,
someone that loves you and will show that they care.
Someone to show that it's truly all love
and what it's really like in that heaven above.

Anger

Anger – that lower place in your soul,
the emotion that stops you from reaching your goal.
Where is it from; what is its game?
Happiness and anger are they the same?
Both are emotions, both are real.
Both are a way of making you feel
that you're still alive, still feeling pain.
But one is a loss and one is a gain.

Never send anger away for good;
it's something that should always be there in your blood.
Just learn to control it and keep it in check
and never allow it to make you a wreck.
Now about happiness what can we say?
Is that an imposter that's just here for today?
It's only around when your life is good
and when it leaves you it goes with a thud.

Is happiness a good friend or just fair weather?
Is it something that should be with you whatever?
Emotions are aliens that play with your heart,
but remember to keep them, you must never part.
Because they are part of your ups and your downs,
they are the cause of your smiles and frowns.
So remember you need them both by your side,
because when they go, that's when you have died.

Can we ever atone?

The light that I see coming in from the rain,
appears much brighter, after that terrible pain.
I'll just close my eyes and let them adjust,
then suddenly I feel a bit of a gust.
The place looks familiar, but then again not,
it is not warm, not cold, it's not even hot.
The sun doesn't shine and yet it's not dim.
But wait, who is that man? Oh, it's my Uncle Jim.

I know he's been dead for a good thirty years,
but the feeling I get, brings me to tears.
What has just happened? I ask like I know.
It was your time, my child, and you had to let go.
The pain and the suffering you previously said
is no longer there as your body has shed.
The earth you can visit, but the first thing you must do
is to adjust to your heaven and everything new.

Soon we will meet the loved ones you mourn
and then you will see that they will no longer scorn.
For they are the same, but the anger they shed,
when they discarded their physical and put it to bed.
The love that you'll feel is like nothing before.
Oh! Here is your cottage, lets walk through the door.

Standing before me was my mum and my dad
and then came the tears - but not cos I'm sad.
The elation I feel fills me with love,
it's true - there really is a heaven above.

But I don't deserve this cos I wasn't good;
I once hit my sister so hard it brought blood.
I stole the milk from the neighbour's step,
and kicked their sheepdog, the one they call Shep.
I once had a fight whilst drunk in a bar
and just to get home – I stole a nice car.

I have been to prison for what I have done,
carried a knife and I've used a gun.
Yes, I did change when I got older.
But do I have the right to stand next to a soldier
that has died for his country and never once moaned?
Yes, said my uncle, because you just atoned.
You remembered the things you did that were bad
and realised they were wrong and it made you sad.
But those that you helped when you were older,
a pauper, a prince and even this soldier.

You see I had a bad chapter and verse,
then I realised my errors and trained as a nurse.
As I was walking home from a bar,
I heard the screeching of a speeding car
and as I turned a child I could see.
And knew that to save him there was only me.
I hastily rushed to move him out of the way,
but the car hit me and then sped away.

For all that I'd done and for all that I've been,
I had just atoned for every sin.
This life I had saved and I never forgot,
His dad years ago was the one that I shot.

Just be yourself

(*Can we ever atone? – part 2*)

What am I good at? I'm asking myself.
If I don't have a skill I'll be left on the shelf.
Shall I join the army? Yes I can't wait.
I could fight for my country, now that would be great,
or perhaps be a milkman – but that's not a trade.
My ideas are already starting to fade.

What can I do, that would make me "kewl"?
For a start I could listen when I go to school.
But it's much more fun to laugh at the teacher.
I'd pinch her bum if I could only reach her.

What can I do to earn me some money?
I could get a job – now wouldn't that be funny?
I'll stay on the dole and work on the side.
When you're making money who needs pride?

What can I do to pull that fit girl?
I could buy her a diamond, some gold or a pearl.
But I can't afford that because I am broke,
so a massage is cheaper, because I'm a bloke.

Why have I wasted all of my life?
I should be rich, with a house and a wife.
I sit in the pub making my pint last
and wonder where the time's gone and think of the past.

What can I do to get me on track?
I want a good job and to get my life back.
Where are my friends that I used to fetch home?
Oh yes, they have jobs and a life of their own.

Why is it easy for others to live?
For any of their lives there's nowt I wouldn't give.
I sit here feeling I've been left on the shelf,
then a voice that I know says "just be yourself".

I quickly turn around but no-one is there.
To be honest it gave me a bit of a scare,
but it did make me think about all that I've been.
And I realised to myself I have to come clean.

Just who is that I am trying to fool?
I've been doing it wrong since I was at school.
Today is the start of the rest of my life;
I will get a job, a house and a wife.

I put down my beer and went home to my mum,
I cried on her shoulder at being so dumb.
How could I be the fool that I am?
I begged for an answer, please tell me mam.

Well, son, I'll tell you now that you ask,
bringing you up was a difficult task.
When you were young you tried to be
somebody else and that I could see.
You tried to be good at not being you,
at being your father that you never knew.
But I love you so much and I'm glad that you cry,
because now you realise where your priorities lie. continued...

She went on to tell me that my dad had been shot
and the gangster that did it had never forgot.
For one fateful day there was this speeding car,
that was going to hit me and she was too far.
But this gangster he saved me and pushed me out of the way,
he said it was his debt that he had been waiting to pay.

How can I fix it and make it all right?
Well, just think about it tonight.
But first I must tell you that the voice that you heard,
was that of your dad – it may sound absurd.
It was something he said to you when you were young,
when he put you to bed and just after he sung.
He truly believed that's all that you need,
to believe in yourself and do a good deed.
For everyone knows that there's no easy way,
that we pay for tomorrow what we do today.

Hello, I am now happy with my good life.
I have a home, a car and even a wife.
All that I did was put my pride on the shelf
and the thing that I'm good at is being myself.
So tell all your young to sit up and learn,
it's respect not cash that we all have to earn.
So stop trying to find what it is you do best,
just be yourself and...

Well, you know the rest.

I want to be me

I often wonder who I'd be,
if I hadn't decided to be me.
Maybe be a boxer or maybe a clown,
or an elegant queen with her regal gown.
I can't decide what it is I'll be
and what I want my people to see.
They'll see me laugh, they'll see me cry,
and then will weep when I die.
Why do we worry about who we are?
and how rich by the type of car?

You see I am a spirit from the other side
and I chose my path till the day I died.
When we're first born we have no thought
about our life, or the happiness sought.
But as we grow we follow our peers,
where politics and religion waste our years.

For we look at man and how we rage,
until we reach a ripe old age.
What is it we seek and why do we look?
It's like our life has to be a book.
Everyone knows the good and the bad
and life in general makes us sad.
But we can laugh and make others smile,
so let's all just do it once in a while.

continued...

Not cos we're spirit and not cos we could,
but just cos we can and to make us feel good.
So next time you're thinking about what you can be,
just think of your world and all that you see.
Take a step back and look at your life,
talk to your children, or husband or wife.
Then look again, at what you really see,
then say to yourself: I just want to be me.

Proof

Can each of us be honest and say that we've been good?
Did our Jesus really die to save our precious blood?
Is there really a spirit world watching as we grow?
Do you think that we can trust? Will we truly ever know?

Can each of us be honest and say we never hate?
Can we stand and say that truth whilst waiting at God's gate?
Say that we have never raged or struck a single blow?
Can we pass without a fault when it's our time to go?

Can we lose a child and never question why?
Is it really there with God, in that place up in the sky?
And then there's war and tragedy – surely that's not fate?
What if when you're dead, you're dead
and there's no-one there to wait?

Why are we so different from others in their quest?
Why should we think our spiritual truth is truer than the rest?
Is my father standing by and helping all the time?
Do I really have inspirers, helping with this rhyme?
Do I really have your mother here proving every fact?
Or is it just a clever ploy, because I've learned to act?

I don't really think so, and let me tell you why.
Why I think our family's there in that heaven in the sky.
I really have my dad here – I feel it in my bones.
Of course, I am not perfect; I have my gripes and moans

continued...

I can truly tell you all that I'm not always good
and I do believe that Jesus died to save our precious blood.
I can't say I've never raged or struck a single blow,
I won't die without a fault when it's my time to go.

I believe the spirit world is there when life is tough,
I know it cos it's in my heart; I believe it – that's enough.
Of course, when someone close is lost,
we lose them when they die,
but only in the physical sense and, of course, we question why.

Truly in our heart of hearts, a spiritualist does know
that you'll always be around and drop by to say hello.
Not because we're fools at all, no we can't stand aloof.
We accept and we know this fact, simply because of proof.

How do we change?

I wonder often when our loved ones pass
if they see things different from a higher class.
For their bodies have shed and also the pain,
leaving that physical for a much higher plane.
To themselves they look at all that they did,
from the day of their passing back to when they were a kid.

For we are not born with a specific mould;
it's habits we gather, as we grow old.
The influence – the lies, the hurt and the pain
are things that we judge on the much higher plane.
Then we can look at the truth of it all,
atone for our sins and then we'll stand tall.
Now just let me say how the spirit world works:
nothing's for free and there's no perks.
All that you get, will be all that you earn
and if you need more lessons, then you can return
to the physical life, but not like before.
It could be a policeman, a lawyer, priest, or a bore.

It all depends on the needs of your soul,
to go to that higher place once you've reached you goal.
But none of it's easy, as I'm sure you will know
by the way your life's been and the way it will go.
Now nothing is planned because of free will,
if we move on, or if we stand still.
It's all up to us with the path that we choose.
Then there's the loved ones we'll ultimately lose.
At that point, we ask why have they gone?
Well their bodies have died and they had to move on.
For now starts again the atonement they seek,
before they come back through a medium this week.

Am I really dead?

Tell me I'm not dead right now,
and this place is just a dream.
Tell me that my wife's downstairs,
making coffee with a lump of cream.
Tell my I'm just panicking because I felt a pain.
Tell me that I can wake up now,
and I'm not going insane.

I don't want to die right now.
I haven't lived my life.
I have my hols to think about
with my children and my wife.
I don't want to say goodbye
to those I love the most.
But wait a minute what's that smell?
I think it's burning toast.

I hear a shout – a familiar voice,
ringing in my ears.
Is this the hope I'm asking for,
the one to take my fears?
Wake up now, your breakfast's done,
do you want coffee with your cream?
It's my wife – thank God I'm still alive,
and this was just a dream.

Believe

Is your heart an organ?
Or a symbol of your love?
The science and the spiritual,
fits us like a glove.
We all need perspective,
something we can touch,
to qualify and quantify,
we need it very much.

It's very hard to comprehend,
a world that's made of light,
shining constantly with beauty
and never having night.
A world with unconditional love
and never knowing loss,
a well-earned rest from a difficult life.
A world without a boss,
our mums, our dads, our nans and gramps.
There, all our loved ones are there,
coming close constantly,
to let us know they care.
If we just took time to feel and know,
how much they endear,
then our world would be a better place,
because we know they're near.

Humankind

The thing with humans is we have so much time
and too many hills that we constantly climb.
Always chasing that faraway goal,
not even realising the needs of our soul.
Unlike the rest of the animal race,

we find it so hard to put a smile on our face.
Take a dog for example, I ask –
that animal is born with one simple task.
To please its master and a tail to wag,
not spending its life thinking: what a drag.

Then look at the fish that swim in the sea,
jumping and diving, living so free.
The birds all around high in the sky,
not even wondering about time passing by.
All of Earth's life except for ourselves,
has no hopes or dreams, nor think of themselves.

They just enjoy life's lie; it's a beautiful gift.
There's no family feuds or marital rift.
They look at the beauty and know nothing of stress,
nor spend all their lives just trying to impress.
So stop for a second, take a leaf from their book,
your life isn't really full of bad luck.

Life's what you make it, warts an' all.
So take a little time to set out your stall,
think of it simply and start it today.
Keep smiling, whatever the rest of 'em say.
For it is your life, don't let it pass by,
take control of it now and aim for the sky.

A healthy mind

There's nothing like a good exercise,
especially when you've just opened your eyes.
Maybe some yoga or even a jog,
to start off your day and oil that cog.
Nothing too heavy if it's not in your norm;
just start off light, the habit will form.

Maybe some weight loss or just for some fun,
your ideas and thoughts come out with a run.
Sometimes our life passes us by,
the years have just gone in the blink of an eye.
But look at the beauty we have all around
and there's even more that you haven't yet found.

Out in the country unspoiled and sweet,
where like-minded people you're likely to meet,
passing the time whilst enjoying the sun.
Life can be simple and still be such fun,
so whatever it is that is getting you down,
the trouble and drama that's making you frown,
take a step back, get some fresh air,
go for a walk, try not to care.
Just for a moment send it away;
it may return but not for today.
Today is the start of the rest of your life,
so live it with beauty, never with strife.

The sceptic

As I describe your husband,
your wife, your mum or gran,
tell you how they lived their life
and how they'll visit when they can,
but that fits anyone you say,
all grans have grey hair,
they grow old and breathless,
there's no evidence there.

I understand your problem
and it's your right not to believe.
But your gran is here today,
the one who watched you grieve.
I'm sorry I'm not different
from all the other grans;
I had grey hair and was very tired
and, yes, I washed the pans.

I did have breathing difficulties
and a problem with my thigh.
Of course, I knew that, one day,
this old body would die.
But I am here in spirit
and I love you oh so much.
And I always promised,
that I would keep in touch.

continued...

Go easy on the medium,
he talks a little quick.
But make sure he describes me well;
if not give him some stick.
He'll get my personality
and some other facts I'll give.
He'll tell you more about my life
and how I used to live.

Take the love I have for you
and, of course, my great advice.
But listen to what I say to him,
because I won't tell him twice.
Yes, all grans are similar
and we sometimes have grey hair,
but sit and listen to me now
and please believe I'm there.

Happy birthday Dad

Hey Dad, happy birthday, you're 82 today.
It's a little over 15 years since God took you away.
I still feel so much sadness and miss you so much more.
I thought I saw you yesterday just standing by the door.

I know it's wishful thinking and you weren't really there,
but your spirit is and that I'm sure because you touched my hair.
We weren't the type to talk of love and didn't say it much,
but I will now: I love you dad, so please just keep in touch.

The road

The road that I travel is a long, long walk,
I need someone with me, so I can talk.
I look to my left and I look to my right
and as quick as I blink the day turns to night.

Now it's not that I'm afraid of the dark,
but I just can't wait for the morning to start.
Cos everything's fresh and it all starts anew
and I only enjoy it because I'm with you.

Now it's not that I'm afraid of being alone;
I just need someone at the end of a phone.
Someone who loves me and listens intent,
when I complain and moan, and never relent.

I look at you sleeping cos that's when you're free,
to spend time with your spirit and not worry about me.
I thank God for spirit that it always survives,
because I want more than the rest of our lives.

Now it's not that I'm greedy, but I think we're soulmates,
I want to go with you past them pearly gates.
We'll walk down that path that God made with love
and see that perfect garden with the white turtle dove.

You may not believe or feel like I do,
but I know together we'll see hard times through.
We shout and we fight, we scream and we moan,
but anything's better than being alone.
We first made our choices before we were born,
to experience life in the physical form.

To look at the tasks that lead us through life
and also to find a good husband or wife.
I talk to you now as if you were here,
cos I cannot bear it and have that great fear.
That I'll wake in the morning and this will be real,
that you're really in spirit and the hurting won't heal.

For all dads

As I woke up this morning,
I thought about my dad.
The times we had together here
were a mix of good and bad.
But looking back upon my life,
I wouldn't change a second,
except that day that broke my heart.
The one where God had beckoned,
that call dad just had to take,
and sadly off he went.
It's at that point we realise,
all the quality times we spent.
So I would like to write this verse,
for those that feel sad,
remember he is with you now.
Happy Father's Day, Dad.

The psychic I went to visit today

You're going to pass I heard her say,
the psychic I went to see today.
Your troubles are over, you'll get a new job,
from now you'll be happy, there's no need to sob.
You'll have three children, two boys and a girl,
your nan brings a gift, a beautiful pearl.
I listen intently to what she has to say,
the psychic I went to visit today.

I must admit it's just 12 o'clock
and I've already had a massive shock.
Then she told me about all my life,
how I was loved by my kids and my wife.
That death is not feared by those who believe;
it's the ultimate goal we all strive to achieve.
Not being morbid but in a spiritual way,
said the psychic I went to visit today.

I went home dazed to my kids and my wife,
to tell what the psychic said of my life.
She stood there a gape at the things that I said,
the poor lady fainted when told I'd be dead.
After a while we sat and we talked,
about all of our life and the places we'd walked.
I'd made sure I provided for my kids and my wife,
so without me they'd still have a wonderful life.

continued...

You see there is something I forgot to say,
I didn't tell the psychic that I went to today.
The doctor had told me after doing the test,
I had two months to live and that was at best.
That terrible illness had come to my home
and gone to my liver, my kidneys and bone.
So, yes, I was shocked at what I heard her say,
the psychic I went to visit today.

I didn't believe in life after death,
it was all stuff and nonsense I told my wife Beth.
Of course, I was scared – I had that great fear,
what would happen when I'm no longer here?
Crying and sobbing whilst lying in bed,
believing that once you are dead, you are dead.
But the things that I heard that good lady say,
the psychic I went to visit today.

She convinced me of heaven that place up above
and how all my family were waiting with love.
So now with some pain and a tear in my eye,
I admit I am no longer too scared to die.
To those spirits that love me
and to my dad Jack,
can you please build my cottage?
Cos I'm on my way back.

Slow down

Now just hold on there, young man,
they're all doing the best that they can.
Life is not one big race,
it's not always something you have to chase.
Everything doesn't have to make you stressed,
you've not got to always prove you're the best.
Take some time to look and see
what the other people see.
It's not all speed and spinning tyres,
that's not what you need to light the fires.
Don't stress yourself from dawn till dark –
to light a fire you just need a spark
and that is what the others possess;
they don't want curses, they want you to bless.

So just slow down – why the push?
Why is your life in such a rush?
Just be calm and take your time,
a poem doesn't have to rhyme.
You don't always have to run
like a bullet from a speeding gun.
Life comes and goes fast enough,
so just slow down, walking's enough.
Remember the tortoise and the hare,
the massive difference in the pair,
but each of them had their line,
they both finished around the same time.
So hear, take heed of what I say,
Rome was not built in a day.

continued...

Take time to work, but time also to play.
So look at your friends, you're not in a race
and just for today, walk at their pace.
No matter what you think of life
and those around you now,
there's always reciprocated love,
it will find you somehow.
There are those around you that you trust
and who will never let you down.
Of course, there's those that make you sad
and who always get you down.
But inwardly we are spirit and don't always see
it's just a life that we're passing through,
it's the same for you and me.

It's circumstance that makes it look
like we are good or bad
and circumstance that changes our view
and make us happy or sad.
So take a look around you now
at those you love or hate.
Then take some time to think again
and let those feelings wait.
For when you're looking from within,
the deep place in your goal,
you'll only find that hating
will leave a great big hole
This is in your heart, that place,
we know when things are right.
So fill it now with lovely thoughts
before you sleep tonight.

Night fears

Is it ghosts or dark I fear
when I hear whispers drawing near?
The memories of times gone by,
flickering shadows that caught my eye.
The shadows in my room at night,
I jump in fear, turn on the light.

But then I couldn't sleep at all,
for different shadows on the wall.
So as I look now full of age,
the still night fears are here to rage.
Sometimes I lay awake at night,
praying for the morning light.
What is that I thought I saw?
Something walking by the door?
Should I stand and try to find,
or is it something in my mind?
I quickly ask my spirit friend,
and pray to God for this to end.

But then I hear a voice inside,
that tells me I don't have to hide.
It's not your mind and it's not bad,
it's only negative when you're sad.
When shadows come you should smile
and then your fear will run a mile.
For what you see and what you hear,
it's just your loved ones drawing near.
Good night my child, I bid you sleep,
and safe and sound we promise to keep.

New Year's Day

New Year's Day and I've just awoken,
sitting alone not a word has been spoken.
Thinking about what this year will bring:
will we cry or will we sing?

It depends on our outlook on life,
the one we share with our husband or wife.
How much we work at making the best,
of what life has to offer, passing that test.

Our family and friends will always be there,
in life and in death so long as we care.
For all of their needs and help when we can
and let our life follow that intricate plan.

The one that we made deep down in our soul
and enjoy the journey until reaching our goal.
Now this may sound crazy but it's what I believe.
When somebody dies, do I not still grieve?

But I do understand and know with my heart,
that true friends and family are never apart.
So think of the hardship you have in your life,
look at your friend or your husband or wife, and
think of those troubled, those with no hope.

Then say to yourself: can I really not cope?
Look in your heart then look up above,
think of the world and send it some love.

All is not lost

I feel a little hot right now, is this my end of life?
How am I going to manage without my kids and wife?
You see I'm ill and there's no hope of me getting well;
I know they know it's time for me, from their face I can tell.
But wait a min' who is that man I think I recognise?
Is that my dad that's standing there? I can't believe my eyes.
It's ok, son, it is your time and I have come to tell you,
that your time is over on this earth, it's been a living hell.

But now your time has ended, there's a special place you'll be;
it is that place you've dreamed about and, yes, it is with me.
Soon you'll meet the family, you've only heard in tales;
Yes, this is heaven that you would call where nothing ever fails.
The stress and the harm that you have seen
can now be left behind;
you can look upon your life and happiness you'll find.
So say goodbye to all these here; it's time to come along.
Yes, time for you to take your place and sing your final song.

You will be back again one day to tell them you are fine,
but just for now relax and sleep and wait here for my sign.
It won't be long, of that I'm sure, and we'll be on our way.
So cry not my child and have no fear upon this special day,
your loved ones are here – they will heal
and know that you are well,
now that you've left this earthly plane, that was your living hell.

Our holiday

The sun is shining, the weather is hot;
I'm sure there's something that I've forgot.
Cases packed, tickets here, looking forward to a beer.
Off to sunny Spain I am,
me, my missus and my mam.
She's never been abroad before,
the furthest she's been is Yorkshire moor.
I ask her if she's feeling well;
you're not nervous are you, Nell?
Of course, I'm not, me mam replied,
I wish we'd done this before John died.
John's my dad, he passed away.
I also wish he was here today,
he died in 1995 – my instinct says he's still alive.

Cos I believe in life after death,
the soul survives after you take your last breath.
He's coming with us, soon we'll be gone
and he won't miss this, not my dad John.
So think about the ones you mourn,
when you see the flowers on the lawn.
On that sad day they're laid to rest,
that is when they're at their best.

For they will know your heart is sad
and that you wish for what you always had.
Of course, they grieve in their own way
that they're not standing with you today.
Well not in the physical – it's that which has died –
but there in the spirit, standing right by your side.
Just take a second and send them your love
and believe that they're safe in that heaven above.

All our troops

It's today that we remember
the soldiers from the war.
Those who died to save our lives.
Yes, those that have gone before.
The brave departed loved ones
that knew they were to die.
Today's when we remember
how quick their time would fly.

As they descend upon us,
bringing peace across the land,
why do mindless bigots
try to make our poppies banned?
The politics, the lies and the hate
is that all that they can give?

To these brave relentless soldiers
that gave their lives so we can live.
So stand up for your country,
stand up for your right.
To wear your poppy with upmost pride
we should all stand up and fight.

Do we have nine lives?

Sitting alone dazed and confused,
is this my last life that I have just used?
The say like a cat, a human has nine.
I'm sure that was the last of mine.
One second I'm walking along with my wife,
when I saw approaching a guy with a knife.
How can I help you? I ask like I know.
Give me your money and then I will go.
Of course, I was willing to give it away,
my fears for my wife were real today.
Then she started screaming cos he'd grabbed her hand –
leave her alone! was my final demand.

I quickly rushed him, seemed the right thing to do,
my only mistake was not thinking it through.
I felt a sharp pain just under my heart,
now I'm watching my wife as we're moving apart.
Things have gone quiet and then came a light,
which was really strange cos I knew it was night.
But that not the weirdest thing, no not by a mile.
It was seeing my father look at me and smile.

Son, just relax because you've just been hurt.
What of my wife? I would scarily blurt.
The lady you love is safe and she's well
and she's just in shock, in her own little hell.
But worry you not, for we have prepared
for her family and friends to stop her being scared.
It suddenly hit me and then became real;
the knife that went through me, I could no longer feel.   continued...

Am I really dead now and is this the place
that everyone talks about and says it is ace?
I'm so pleased to see you, but can't help being sad,
will this ever get better? I'm asking my dad.
Walk with me son, so we can chat,
the lives thing you think is not the same as the cat.

Your bodies are weak and easy to tear,
from the soles of your feet to the top of your hair.
You must be careful of the actions you take,
think of the decisions that you'll have to make.
The reason for living on this violent earth
has not yet been realised.
You still have a birth,
the child you will have will help with world peace.
It won't make it perfect but some wars it will cease.
Your act of pure bravery you take for your wife,
was lovely but silly and it could take your life.

The sudden realisation of what he's just said,
hit me like a bullet – so am I not dead?
As much as I'll miss you, it's just not your time,
so go back my child, right back to the crime.
Don't be so hasty and don't be so rash,
if a man has a weapon just hand him your cash.
It's not really worth it, cos you have your task.
But what shall I say about you if they ask?
Just tell them your father is safe in this place
and once you come over, it will be so ace.
Be sure all the tasks are done in your life
and, for God's sake, just keep away from the knife.

Rainbows

Am I chasing rainbows?
That is how I feel,
it's like the hopes and dreams I have
are not actually real.
So what's in store? I ask myself.
What am I to do? Should I give it one more year?
Or maybe another two?

What could happen in that time
and what could I expect?
I think I've had plenty of time
to look back and reflect.
Could I do things differently
or would I be the same?
This small dilemma I am in
is really such a shame.

So then I ask myself again
if I should chase that dream.
All I'm doing at this time is living out a theme,
the same as everyone I know
walking on this earth,
that we are going to be great someday.
We've had it since our birth.

continued...

I think that what I'm saying is,
YES chase that rainbow there.
Of course, you will not catch it
and life just isn't fair.
So don't just stand there moping
and asking questions why.
Grab your hopes and dreams right now
and aim them at the sky.

Little Bean

Dedicated to Natalie and Ian

Hello my girl – my little bean,
it's really nice to see
that you've been growing all this time,
that you've been part of me.
We've so been looking forward to your arrival in our fold,
we had so much to teach you, girl,
and some loving arms to hold.

But, sadly, it's not meant to be, God has chosen your fate –
back into his arms you go, right back to his gate.
Sometimes angels are not meant to walk upon this earth
and this is why I carried you – but didn't go full birth.
The love I feel is now well matched with sadness in my heart
that we can never be together – we have to be apart.
I know you'll be there by my side, walking hand in hand.
I don't know why God took you back – I just can't understand.

Is it really selfish that I want you for myself?
To look at clothes and buy the toys that I see on the shelf?
Yes, I wanted to be proud of you, my little bean,
to walk around with all the mums,
to be special and to be seen.
I saw you in my dreams last night and kissed you on the cheek.
It made me cry and laugh so much,
because I heard you speak.
Now these fine words I have to share with the entire world today,
the words I heard so clearly were:
Mum, I'll never go away.

Xmas Eve

It is Xmas Eve tomorrow,
the snow is on the ground.
I have mixed feelings nowadays,
when Xmas comes around.
It's not that I'm a humbug
or scrooged in any way.
It's just I wish the others were with us here today.
My dad's been gone for 15 years
and it's one for Karen's mum.
It grieves my heart and makes me cry
to know this time has come.

I want to laugh, I want to cry,
I want to hug my wife.
We think we'll be together
the rest of each other's life.
But God has other plans, you see,
and takes them on their way.
I pray to him to take no more,
starting from today.
The place that God will take them
is heaven, as you know,
and that's the place that we call home,
when it is our time to go.
So love your family and your friends
and treat them all with care.
There may just be a little chance,
that soon they won't be there.

Another Xmas Eve

Xmas Eve where we all wind down,
pick up those last pressies from the town.
Defrost the turkey in the sink,
serve it piping, but a little pink.
Xmas Eve have an early dart,
for your colleagues and company you've done your part.
Stand in a queue for over an hour,
for the last-minute smellies
that she takes to her shower.
Xmas Eve wrap the last of the toys,
wishing we were still little girls and boys.

Xmas Eve where the lonely and poor,
live on the streets frozen to the core.
Xmas Eve a time to be nice,
think of the homeless out there in the ice.
Xmas Eve we're safe behind our door,
think of our soldiers fighting the war.
Send out a blessing, take a minute to pray,
that all of God's creatures have a lovely Xmas Day.

It's only text

Has the world gone mad arguing and fighting?
Taking offence to what someone is writing.
Text is viewed according to your mood;
it doesn't mean to say the writer is rude.
Facebook can build and make some good friends,
but it's also responsible for some tragic ends.
So when you come on and see what is wrote,
don't just dive in like a mad billy goat.
Read it out loud and speak in your mind,
read it again and see if it's kind.
Don't create drama if it does offend,
just go to your profile and click on unfriend.

I've had enough

Twas the night before Xmas and most were in bed,
Mum was up cooking, Dad stoned off his head.
Fetch me a lager and a joint he would shout,
or I'll wake up the kids an I'll give 'em a clout.
Ok, my dear, says the wife in a rush,
puffing and panting and feeling quite flush.
Anything else you would like from the shelf?
If you do, you fat bastard, then get it yourself.

For I am just leaving, kids already gone,
the only food left is a fat mouldy scone.
So happy Xmas, you fat ugly drunk,
I never could stand you, you smell like a skunk.
Don't even think Santa will come here tonight,
for you it's a no-no, he's just taken flight.
Xmas is special for me though, she said,
cos I'm off to his grotto and then straight to his bed.

It's war again

There are those that turn and run away,
that live to fight another day.
Then the ones that start a war
and learned no lessons from the one before.
Those in power making decisions,
telling the world of their peaceful visions.
My word is God, don't come to my town,
if you look at me wrong – I will strike you down.

Jobless and wounded our soldiers return
to the angry world with a possible spurn.
You've done your job and thanks very much
but now I'm too busy to keep in touch.
I'm busy preparing to even the score
with another great country, this could be war.

So now starts the cycle, call the women and men
to do what they must and go fighting again.
What is it for this time? we may ask.
It's not your concern, just get on with the task.
We then look to space, the final frontier –
are we alone, the only ones here?
We look to the planets for other signs of life,
somewhere away from the trouble and strife.
Then come the words that we know oh so well –
what if they're hostile, how can we tell?

We can build lasers and guns to defend.
On this day, we remember those who fell,
those loved ones who braved it. I'm sure they could tell
that those they were fighting all had family too.
They fought for their country, not what they knew.

It's probably for land, religion or hate.
If only our leaders could stop and just wait,
just for a second think of the brave,
then just talk it over – how many lives that would save?
Learning to love and just understand
is a difficult lesson that we all have at hand.
Let's give it a try, just for today,
and see how our wars will just melt away.

For Queen and country

Is this for my country that I stand and fight?
And not even consider as to whether it's right?
I am a soldier and have been for a while;
I sometimes find it hard to just smile.
For what I have done and what I have seen
has been for the love of my country and Queen.
So just take a minute and please bow your head
for those brave ones before me
who's names shall be read.

Mediums

Many mediums have ups and down.
Some readings bring smiles,
some will bring frowns.
Assess your life and where it will go.
Will you carry on? Only you will know.

What are we doing? Serving the soul?
What is you aim? And what is your goal?
Yes, it is sometimes a thankless task.
Is it all worth it? we constantly ask.
It's not like giving up if you just stop;
it's just making time to nip down the shop.
Clean up the house, do that old chore,
things that the normals consider a bore.

When I say normals – it's those with a life,
those that spend time with their husband or wife.
It's not that I hate it or think it's one sided,
I just think that sometimes our life is divided.
Between the two worlds is where we stand aloof,
trying to reach that spiritual truth.

continued...

So look at your life, your family and friends,
think of it all and when your time ends.
Did you spend all of it trying to prove
that spirit's around you and will never move?
Or did you go out and just have a good time,
enjoying good food and drinking good wine?
Whatever you choose has to come from your heart
and if it's not Spiritualism, then you've still done your part,
simply because you chose your goal
and remembered to follow just what's in your soul.

Boxing Day

Well, Boxing Day it is today,
on the floor the presents lay.
Paper scrunched up in the bin,
right beside the turkey skin.
All the sprouts have done their part
and made the smelly family fart.
Today's the day to gather round,
the day that family come around.

Eat the curry from the pan,
lots of turkey and cranberry jam.
Talk about the ones not here,
the ones we miss so close and dear.
All in all, it's a happy crowd,
dancing and laughing and singing aloud.
Of course, the songs are not in tune,
I think my ear drum will burst real soon,
so time to finish off this rhyme.

Clean the house so it's looking fine,
cook the food they're going to eat.
Then, just relax in my favourite seat,
watch a bit of Dr Who,
while wife makes brekky and a lovely brew.
Merry Xmas, although it's gone,
and I hope your Boxing Day's a beautiful one.

The circle of light

It's getting near Xmas on a cold Thursday night
and I am at Wallasey doing the circle of light.
It's a far far cry from when I was young,
cos Xmas was about boring hymns that were sung.

About a child that was born with God as his dad.
I always thought Mary had done something bad.
I couldn't get round this miracle birth
and strangers brought presents – gold, frankincense and myrrh.

But distracted I was with the toys in my bag,
I'd sit there excited while dad had his fag.
Go on then, lad, unwrap if you like.
My excitement was worth it – he'd bought me a bike.

I looked at my sister and she had a pram,
that was a present that was bought by my mam.
Christmas was simple cos I was a kid,
I remember the excitement of all that we did.
Snakes and Ladders and Ludo, of course,
until it was time for dad to bet on his horse.

Then off we'd go to our friends. We would boast,
while mam set about doing the great Xmas roast.
Crackers we'd pull to put on our hat
and out popped a toy, a little black cat.

Xmas in the seventies was great as a kid.
I remember the neighbour the guy called Sid.
He'd make us toys out of old wood with his tools,
as long as we were good and obeyed all his rules.
Don't make noise cos I'm on regular nights,
be good little children, don't get into fights.

As I sit here writing this rhyme,
I remember so many things about that time.
All the sweets they had in the shops,
the sherbet fountains and the fab lollipops.

Satsumas and nuts in your Xmas bag,
a nice pack of Chewits and a candy fag.
So back to this evening, the circle of light
and what it's about – this beautiful night.

It's all about you – yes, you people here,
the ones that are singing and bringing good cheer.
It's not just the pressies, although they are "kewl"
and that juicy turkey that makes us all drool.

We should spare some thoughts for those who are sad,
the ones who are ill and those who are bad.
Just say a prayer for the whole world tonight,
pray for world peace and for no-one to fight.
Don't forget healing to be sent on its way
and Xmas for all, a beautiful day.

Being yourself

There are those things we cover up
and hide from all our friends.
That feeling of fragility in our life that never ends.
Just be tough we tell ourselves – keep on that brave face.
Be big and strong just like our kin that we have to replace.
Don't be you, be like them, we always tell our mind,
keep your pride within reach where you can easily find.

But let me tell you here, right now – doing that is tough,
being someone you are not means you're living on the cuff.
Why can't we just all be calm and live a life of peace,
a life of love and solitude, that lets our stress decrease?
So from now on, just be yourself. It's all that you can be.
Don't get drawn into the world that others want to see.
For that's when time is not our own – we've given it to our past.

And happiness for that short time we know can never last.
Live in the world where you can smile
and be happy with your life.
That place that you are comfortable,
the one without the strife.
Understand where this place is
and that it's where you should be.
Then stand up high and shout out loud,
I'm happy to be me.

It's just how I feel

The way that I am feeling, I am not a happy guy.
I am thinking to the spirit world
of saying thank you and goodbye.
I try to be a medium and try to be just me,
but after all the work I've done, I have gone back to I.T.
Now, I know it's not a bad thing
and balance is what we seek.
But just for once in my whole life,
I would like to have a good week.
It is a thankless job sometimes,
talking to the dead,
telling all your audience,
what you have here in your head.

They just sit with a blank long face, waiting for their turn
and then they leave with not one thanks.
It makes my stomach churn,
so thank you spirit, but no thanks.
As I already said, I think my days are numbered
where I'll be talking to the dead.
I didn't want world riches or fame, no none of that.
All I wanted from you was to help me wear a hat.
One that tells me who I am,
not who I should be.
So goodbye spirit off I go,
right back to I.T.

Salt of the Earth

Now just who are they - the salt of the earth?
The brilliant, the beautiful, right from their birth.
Natural born mediums that talk to the dead,
telling us everything our loved ones have said.
Feeling the passion we thought that was gone,
helping our spirit to accept and move on,
because we all know that our soul never dies.

And spirit can see us and hear all our cries,
so why is it hard for us to see that it's real?
We know we can't touch and we know we can't feel.
Well, not with our hands, well, at least, not just yet.
But we are all progressing, so let's not forget
that this salt of the earth, who talks to our dad,
are not all con artists and not all that bad.

Let's hope that one day that corner we'll turn
and pick up that lesson - spirit wants us to learn.
Then comes the time we'll need mediums no more;
we'll see spirit ourselves, over there by the door.
For that's when it's time for us to leave this great earth
and find our own paradise we've been seeking since birth.

Can there be peace?

What is this world doing fighting in our wars?
Killing, maiming every day, just like the years before.
How can we, as Spiritualists, make our leaders talk?
So our soldiers turn around and right back home they walk.
Then there's all the violence in our homes and on the street.
How can we raise our children to walk proudly on their two feet?

And whilst we're putting the world to rights,
there's hunger and there's drought.
There's so much wrong about the world,
it makes me want to shout.
But who am I to speak like this,
what gives me or you the right?
Just how do we think the world
can safely sleep at night?
We have our everyday life
to deal with as we can,
not poke our nose in other things;
it must be our God's plan.

Or why else would mankind do this,
destroy their life on earth?
It's says our life is all planned out
right back from our birth.

continued...

But is that really how it is?
Surely we can change?
Make this world a better place,
have the power to re-arrange.
So let's all stick together
and say our prayers tonight.
Pray for health and pray for peace,
so we never have to fight.

My Christmas poem

Well, it's here again today,
that good old Xmas Eve.
The last few hours of work to do,
before its time to leave.
Go home, prepare the turkey,
put the presents in the sack.
Sit and think of the good old days
and wish you could go back.
But these are just your memories,
something you hold dear.
Think about your loved ones now
and feel them drawing near.

Pray for peace and happiness
and for all the wars to stop.
And that everyone across the world,
can afford to go and shop.
Just for the essentials
and a little something nice,
that special Xmas pressie
that doesn't have a price.
The one you give with love,
it's given from your heart.
So make Christmas special this year –
everyone can play their part.

Whoops

As I was walking down the street,
feeling tired and incomplete, feeling sad and insecure,
wondering what today will have in store,
I stopped and turned to the voice I heard.
The person I saw was a little blurred.
I walked back so I could see
because I'm nosey – well, that's just me.
As I got close I wasn't so sad
for what I was seeing was my own dad.

He's been dead for many years,
so you can just imagine all the tears.
He told me he hadn't died at all,
he was always there, waiting for my call.
But I never called you, I had to say,
I was just feeling sad and going my own way.
My everyday life has been such a strain
and on my family I had been a drain.

But now I can see you and ask your advice,
maybe my life now will be nice.
In one way it will, son, but some things I must say,
now you have to listen as it's just for today.
Whilst you were walking with your head in the cloud,
ignoring the car that was beeping so loud,
a little too late – no time for delay,
for the driver to stop or get out of the way.

You feel no pain cos your spirit we caught
but you have hurt your leg, I have to report.
What am I doing I suddenly think,
am I going to die – my dad gave me a wink.

With a familiar smile, that big cheeky grin,
the one that I recognised,
when a good mood he was in,
put his hand on my shoulder, which felt really nice,
it was very warm and as cold as ice.
No, son, today we were there for your soul,
as your life's not finished, you've not reached your goal.
A medium is what you have set out to be,
do it with happiness, do it for me.
You will be the best and you'll do it with love,
you talk to the heavens, those loved ones above.

You can't change the world but love you can bring,
so your life is not over 'til the fat lady can sing.
So get back in your body, be happy my son,
keep smiling, LOVE YOU and try to have fun.
Love all your family, your kids and your wife,
remember they also deserve a good life.
But most of all remember this day
and know that your dad has not gone away.
I am just through the door, the one on the right
and I'll keep and protect you every night.
For that's what we're here for – our life never ends.
I love you my son and we will always be friends.

Questions

What are you doing in the spirit world?
What's it like in that place? Will I ever hold your hand?
Will I ever see your face? Do you have a job there dad,
    working for the good?
Did Jesus really die to save our precious blood?

There are so many questions that we have in our mind.
Would the answers that you give benefit mankind?
I just want to talk to you, nothing too profound,
feel your touch, know your love and hear your lovely sound.
To know your wisdom now you're there,
just to know that you still care.
Can you hear the words I say?
Dad, I love and miss you,
Happy Father's Day.

I have changed somehow

I'm not the man I used to be, I think I've changed somehow.
I got a job and found a trade, that's what I'm doing now.
Ten years ago and on the dole, I had a little thought,
I went to college learnt a trade and computers I was taught.
My first job came and then some more, learning was my aim.
I started to enjoy myself, think I like this game.
What made me do this, I don't know, I'd never done before.
I always thought to have a job would be a real chore.
But ten years on, I'm working hard and look back on the dole.
I do still have a way to go before I reach my goal,
but looking now at what I have and how I feel now,
I know one thing that is for sure, I have changed somehow.

The light is different

The light is different somehow, I cannot see the sky,
that heavy body full of pain that now appears to fly.
It's just a dream, I tell myself, for I can't even walk.
I don't want to wake up, I don't even want to talk.
The illness that's within me would never go away,
so tell me why I've never felt as good as I do today.
This place is like a dream to me, so beautiful and calm,
the sort of place to feel safe, you'll never come to harm.
The streets are filled with flowers, an abundance of each kind.
Just how powerful is this dream to do this to my mind?

But wait a min' I look around and who do you think I saw?
No, it's not my wife and kids who I knew were there before.
It's my dad, you know,
    and since he left I've known not what to say,
I've grieved for him constantly since he went away.
I've come to greet you, he said so calm,
I've come to take you home.
It's important at this time for you to know – you're not alone.

So many people in the world carry so much doubt.
Religion's there to comfort you, but most will cast you out.
So put aside all your doubts and the prejudice of man,
walk with me for a while and I'll tell you what I can.
Your suffering is over and all your pain has cleared;
it's not a dream you're having now
and there's nothing to be feared.
Your body died but not your mind, your spirit's living on
and you are in your rightful place, your new life's just begun.

From now on all thoughts are pure and life is full of light,
for all of those you've left behind, let them say goodnight.
Of course, you know you'll never part
    because of your true love
and now they know you're safe and well
    in that spirit world above.

A friend is a friend

We think that there is always time, for us to put things right
things we say to hurt each other when we argue and fight.
The days roll on, the months, the years and nothing else is said,
then one sad and fateful day, one of us is dead.

The memories come flooding back. What was it all about?
That single night so long ago when we felt we had to shout.
We can't even remember really what we did or said,
but we should have let it pass and slept on it in our bed.

It's easy just to disagree and then not speak for years,
but death comes when you least expect
then you're fighting back the tears.
All the hurt and pain we felt, that's all in the past.
Friendship is the only word, something that should last.
But we are stubborn, that's who we are
and sometimes that is good,
but not when time evades that trait
and you lose that friend for good.

So here's a lesson we should learn, for me it is too late.
No matter who is in the wrong, you or your best mate,
just agree to disagree – say sorry if you must.
Give them all of your respect and don't betray their trust;
they are your friend, your guidance,
your conscience and your strength.
A bond that you must always keep, go to any length.
Sometimes we don't see their love, or their heart of gold.
They have gone before their time,
when they should be growing old.

Your friend can be your family, or someone that you know.
It's all the same emotion to have to watch them go.
It breaks your heart, it makes you cry, so sad to see them pass,
that person that you loved so much was in a different class.
So don't be hard or blame yourself; this is part of life,
whether it's your best friend, your husband or your wife.
Speak your mind, say your peace, for that is part of you.
Then once it's said, just let it go, then sit and have a brew.
There's no need for anger or to shout or moan,
all that you end up with is too much time alone.
Put your pride upon the shelf, say sorry to your friend
and then you won't be lonely; they'll be with you to the end.

You've pooped yourself

Snow has fallen on the ground,
beneath our feet that crunching sound.
All of a sudden you start to slide
and now begins your Xmas ride.
Not the type you'd hoped I think,
but either way you're gonna stink.
Those lovely clothes you bought off the shelf,
will have to be changed cos you've pooped yourself!

You left me

I don't really care what tomorrow brings,
whether I wake and hear the birds sing.
I don't really care if you love me or not,
or if you remember or if you've forgot.
I couldn't care less if I live or die
and you're not here to even ask why.
You've left me forever and don't even care
that I'll never kiss you, or brush your grey hair.
You said you'd be here for all of my life,
for better or worse, when I made you my wife.

Now that you've gone, there's something I lack.
I wish I could join you or that you'd come back.
They keep on saying that I just have to feel;
this spirit world thing is supposed to be real.
Why can't I see you, if you're really there.
If I could see you, I think I would care.
They try to tell me that's not how it is,
there's love I can give with an etherical kiss.

So if I calm down and open my mind
and route in my heart what will I find.
Will you be there or will there be nowt?
Maybe one day, I'll be calm and find out.
They say I'm too angry; I shouted I'm not.
You're in my dreams, I think about you a lot.
I just don't get what they mean when they say
that you're always with me and won't go away.

continued...

If you just show yourself one more time,
maybe I'll forgive you and then I'll be fine.
Forgive you for what though? that's what I ask.
I'm feeling so angry it would be a big task.
For now I'll just have to get on with my life,
but one thing's for sure: I'll miss you, dear wife.

Mind your tongue

What was it I said today that made them all so mad?
I didn't really mean to have the argument we had.
All I did was speak my mind and what I had to say.
They walked away so angry and said that I will pay.
I guess I'll have to wait a while and see what they will do,
or maybe they will just calm down
    once they've thought it through.

Some will take your literal words and mix them in their head
and once they've mixed 'em up so much,
they'll wish that you were dead.
There's nothing we can do to change
what is in someone's thoughts.
It's not our job, so just don't try – that is what we're taught.
But life goes on; we're not the same, we think our different ways,
so never try to change someone – you'll just waste all your days.
Spend your time constructively, don't let your life be dull,
and when it's time to go, at least you've lived it to the full.

Egypt

Up bright and early and getting equipped
for today is the day that we go to Egypt.
Feeling excited, needing a poo,
I must stop writing and visit the loo.
So my dear friends, who are lying in bed,
I bid you farewell as I fly over your head.

In my 767 – yes, that's my plane –
as I travel to sunshine and leave you in rain.
I'll think of you often as I lie on the sand,
grinning and smirking with JD in hand.

So off I must go and prepare for my trip
and just as I leave I will give you one tip:
take an umbrella cos rain ain't much fun
and I'll think of you smiling as I lie in that sun.

God

You know the time you talk to God is when you want the light,
but think about the good in him especially when you fight.
For then the anger takes a hold and makes you show your hate –
one day it will consume you all and then it'll be too late.

There's always hope, just so you know. Don't let it go that far.
You're never forced to pray to God, just be the way you are.
Everything is down to you, the way that you react.
The path you walk is all your choice and that, my friend, is a fact,
but if you need a little help, just give him the nod.
You know the one we talk about, the one we call our God.

Finding peace

I've never been a fighter, except for in my head,
mulling over something bad that someone else has said.
Thinking how very wrong they are
and that they should think once more
and only then will I forgive and let them through my door.
I'm very unforgiving with most things in my life;
I'm angry at my family, my children and my wife.
I'm angry at the media and the man who reads the news;
I'm angry when I wake up after a long and peaceful snooze.

So tell me how to change, I ask the angel at my bed.
Of course, I don't believe in you,
     cos once you're dead, you're dead.
I must be drunk or dreaming, cos I blink and you don't go,
so come on now, if you are real, speak and say hello.
I pinch myself to see if this is truly something real.
I guess it is, cos that pinch hurt; that's real pain I feel.
Have you come to take me, and do our souls live on?
Or are you here to help me forgive things and move on?

I feel emotion in my heart, a kind of a release,
then I start to cry a lot. Am I finding peace?
The angel spoke to me these words, which now I will repeat,
I sat and listened carefully as she stood there at my feet.

Young man, this is your chance right now
     to change the way you see,
to tell yourself about your life and how happy it can be.
There are many people suffering across the world you live,

compassion and understanding is all you have to give.
You can't change people's mind or tell them how to live,
the only thing that you can do is learn how to forgive.
Think about humility and keep it in your heart,
trust the love we have for you and know we'll never part.
Ask for things that you desire, that bring love to your life
and then we'll help you love the world
and help you grieve your wife.

I don't know what you're saying now. My wife is lying here.
I know that I don't show it much but I do love her dear.
I don't know what you mean when you're saying I will grieve –
my wife's loves me so much right now,
    I know she'll never leave.

Your wife's been ill for some time now but never has revealed
that pain she's had for two years now just could not be healed.
So I am here to take the pain and her into my wing,
so she can be at peace with us and learn again to sing.

I don't know what you're saying still.
    Are you telling me she's died?
She was not in pain, she said; I know she never lied.
She knew how sad you were feeling at the time that she was ill
and thought you may get angry
    if you knew this disease would kill.
And so she kept it quiet so not to make you upset.
I have take her with me now so please do not forget.

continued...

We are always here for you and so will be your wife,
to help you and to guide you through the rest of your life.
But understand these words, young man:
    I say this from my heart,
your wife will never truly leave and your love will never part.
The physical loss that you will feel will eventually subside
and you will come to realise that your loved one never died.

Yesterday

In the old days things were different, we used to have more fun.
There seems to be change today in how most things are done.
Mam would send us to the shop for something on the bill,
and we could walk for miles and miles cos we had time to kill.
We'd walk across the many fields,
jump from trees onto bales of hay.
I wish our kids could see the fun that we had in our day,
but kids today are different, or is it how I see it?
I just don't think that they could possibly have as much fun as me.

I remember in the 70s there wasn't many cars
and we could safely cross the road and Guy Fawkes outside bars.
The nearest thing we got to games was playing draughts with dad,
and it did no harm to get a slap, but only when we were bad.
We did bag school, that means "not go"
    for those not from our street
and you could walk most anywhere with nothing on your feet.

So what can I remember looking back upon my life?
Well, my dad was still alive back then and doted on his wife.
Yes, they had their rows, I think, but that's how it was,
but understand, Mam made it clear she deffo was the boss.
So how is all that different to life I see today?
Well, kids for sure have no idea what it's like to play.
They're either on their Facebook or playing gory games,
piercing holes into their face, or damaging their veins.
I suppose to them it's normal, so there's nothing I can say
except I'd love to bring to them a little of yesterday.

Spirit Dad

I know that I am Spirit and happy I should be,
but I so want to be with you like you would be with me.
It is just like they say it is, it's full of love and light,
but what I'd give to sit with Nell and maybe spend the night.
I love and miss her oh so much and visit every day.
I still regret so much that time I had to go away.
Why does it still hurt, I ask, after all these years,
surely there should be an end to that massive tank of tears.

A spirit isn't supposed to cry, they don't really have the need,
so let me tell you this, my son, we're here to plant that seed.
To let you see the real side of all things that are love
and let you know just how it is in this heaven up above.
I work with you so much you know and help you every day,
but when I see your mum, my wife, I really want to stay.
They say it's easy from this side to mend that broken heart,
but let me tell you once again, it hurts to be apart.
The only consolation and, yes, this is a lot,
we do meet all the loved ones, even those that we'd forgot.

To put things in perspective so that we understand,
we cannot come through all the time, not just on demand.
We do all have our jobs to do, although they're not like yours,
but every Sunday at the church,
    we'll all walk through those doors.
Then we'll all stand in a line to talk to those that come
and give a little inspiration through that lovely Medium.
We do receive the healing thoughts, so always send them out.
The thoughts turn into energy, we see them all about.

We try to help all those we can, the ones that are so ill
and you don't always have to ask, we know it is your will.

There are certain things that you can ask and we will try to do,
but when there's physical pain you feel,
    we try to get you through.
Of course, there are times we fail and the body needs to die;
it is that time the spirit leaves, you have to say goodbye.
So don't you worry, don't you fret and think that I am sad,
I just want express the love that's coming from your Dad.

Where's the Xmas spirit gone

Where's the Xmas spirit gone?
Oh it's over there.
It's in my mum and in my dad who's sitting on the chair.
Dad will wear his paper crown and pull a Xmas cracker,
he'll roll a ciggie from his tin of old Holborn tobacco.
Then we'll settle down for the main meal of the day
and mum will do the washing up then put the stuff away.
We'll all sit down arm in arm and watch the royal speech,
the Queen addresses the Commonwealth,
a few million she will reach.
Then it's Star Wars, Doctor Who or a girlie flick,
it doesn't matter, it's Xmas day, whichever one you pick.
Of course, this poem isn't true,
as some loved ones are not here,
but it's Christmas, I'm allowed to dream,
Merry Xmas and Happy New Year.

A message from Dad

On that sad day I had to leave,
whilst you went to the bookies to retrieve
my winnings from horses that I chose,
the amount was wrong and everyone knows.

When you came back I'd nearly gone,
you tried to revive me but as time went on
I slipped into that big deep sleep,
but know this Nell, I saw you weep.

They all thought that you were strong,
but I knew that they were wrong.
Now I'm here I watch and learn,
for the family's love I have to earn.
It doesn't come free because we are kin,
but it does in the spirit that we have within.
I see how the days make you forget,
but there are memories to come that you haven't had yet.

I know on the earth our love wasn't strong,
but deep in our spirit, we both had that bond.
For we were together for all of them years,
and as I look back I remember your tears.
I wasn't that good a husband or dad,
but Nellie, my love, I wasn't that bad.

continued...

It's the habits we get as we go through our lives
and unfortunately pass these things on to our wives.
But now I can see all the wrong that I did,
I can be that great husband and a dad to our kids.
I try to guide from this world that I live,
but the focus I give is just on one kid.
The others I love, but they'll have to wait, cos
their time will come, when they open their gate.

Now back to my wife, who I love very much.
I long for your love, your kiss and your touch.
I know that you think about me a lot,
but know this, my Nell, I have never forgot.
Those words that we spoke on our great wedding day
they will never fade away.
'Til death do us part, to cherish and love,
until we meet again in that heaven above.

Yesterday I died again

Yesterday I died again, but this time it was real,
my body and soul did part, now I can start to heal.
It's a little strange to tell the truth. I can't describe my mind.
I'm now in heaven, or so they say. I've left the human kind.
So what's it like? I hear you ask. Is Elvis up there too?
He may well be but not sure where; I'll have a look for you.

The first thing that I felt, of course, was feeling tired and weak,
I think my dad was here as well; I thought I heard him speak.
I look around. It looks the same, but brighter and more clean.
In fact, it is the brightest place that I have ever seen.

The air is clear, the flowers bright, the fruit tastes fresh and sweet,
then I saw something here that knocked me off my feet.
As I was walking down the road to look at my new home,
I saw my dad with Karen's mam, but she was on the phone.
I stood a gasp at what I saw and thought how could this work,
they grinned, of course – the phone's not real.
You believed it though, you berk.
Not lost your sense of humour then, I jokingly replied.
That's one thing we keep, he said,
when our physical body's dead.

Why?

Why is there such anger about religion, race or creed?
Why is our world today about selfishness and greed?
Why can't we just live as one and stop our gripes and moans?
Why do we all spend our time talking on our phones?
Why are we not happy unless there's someone else in pain?
Why for every good person do we have to find a stain?
Why can we just not accept the varieties on this earth?
And that we all are different from the moment of our birth?

For when to this world we are born, there's nothing in our mind,
but innocence, wonder, a mother's love, YES that's what we find.
We don't see religion, race or the colour in your skin.
Those will come at a later time; it's the world we're living in.
So let's just look at where we are and how we all can change,
let each of us have our own style and never think it strange.

Don't condemn that ignorance; some would say it's bliss.
Don't slap their face or turn away; greet them with a kiss.
Let acceptance start with you, and let the whole world know,
that there's no anger with you now,
because you just let it go.

Why do you meditate?

Why do you meditate and listen but not hear the words I say?
Do you believe that I am different since the time I went away?
Do you think that I'm an angel with lovely feathered wings?
Do you think you have special privileges
    with magic that an angel brings?
Why do you meditate and listen and not feel the love I give?
Do you think it just comes naturally, that
    I'll show you how to live?
Do you think my heart is bigger now
    and that maybe it's all or you?
Do you think that I will guide you and show you what to do?

Well, now let me tell you that all your thoughts are right.
Yes I'll protect and love you and guide you
    through your darkest nights,
all you have to do now is ask and I'll be there.

Standing at the window or sitting in my favourite chair.
It's not because you're asking,
    or that you have that special glow.
It's because I truly love you, I'm hoping that you know,
But let me tell you this right now: I love everyone the same
whether you think you have no life, or if you're seeking fame.
Of course, you are not measured by
    the achievements made on earth;
it's the love you have for others
    that was given naturally at birth.

continued...

So now when you meditate and listen,
　　you don't have to try too hard,
you don't need to have a privilege or a special 'love me' card.
I'll be there, I'm just a thought, a feeling that you get
And, of course, I haven't changed, I still like the odd bet.
So if I was to come to you the favour I would ask
is that you enjoy your life, don't make your love a task.
Follow your path, make just sure it is what you desire,
do it well, the best you can, it's yourself you have to admire.
Keep your pride, your head held high, feet firmly on the earth,
for I'll be there right by your side, just as I was from birth.

Where am I going?

Where am I going this year?
What are these thoughts in my head?
Will I go back to computers?
Or spend it talking with the dead?

Will I ever be a great Medium?
Like those I've read in the books.
Is it down to dedication?
Or is it down to luck?

I sit and I ponder for hours
at who are the guides in my life.
Of course, I am talking spiritually
and not of the guide who's my wife.

So back to my plan for this year,
is it world domination for me?
I really don't think it will happen,
that couldn't happen to me.

Why should I think I am special?
Why should I think I am great?
To stand with the big names in spirit,
large audiences I could elate.

Proud like the late and great Gordon,
talk like it's something I know.
Can I ever reach that high standard,
or is this a dream I will have to let go?

continued...

Hold on there Pete, says my guide,
stop doubting your spirit and love.
I'm not just here for a cheap ride,
I am from heaven above.

Listen to what I am saying,
work hard on what you can achieve.
Don't ever doubt your commitment,
don't let your confidence leave.

It's not all about fame and fortune,
nor whether you're on the TV.
It's about feeling it all in your spirit
and you saying I want to be me.

So don't let your thoughts wander too much,
don't let your heart freeze and break.
Just be yourself in your lifetime
and choose all the roads you will take.

That's who you are in this great shell
and nothing within you should change.
Your life will be all that you make it
and then your goals will be all in your range.

What sort of Medium am I?

What sort of spiritual person am I?
Do I actually bring comfort or is it a lie?
Those loved ones that grieve for the loss and the pain
and only through me can they meet them again.
So this is my pledge to those who I see:
I will never lie or pretend, no not me.
It's not in my nature, it's not who I am,
I do it for love and just cos I can.

I'll always be truthful and know what I feel
is that love of the spirit I know to be real.
I am a Medium and I know why you're sad,
cos I am still hurting for the loss of my dad.
When I sit alone, I feel that pain
that I know I will never see him again.
But what gives me comfort in my times of deep hurt
is that fact he's around and that is a cert.
Why do I trust in this thing that I preach?
Cos with feeling and emotion it's what I can teach.

Everyone has it, this gift that's so rare,
but some just ignore it and forget it is there.
Why do they do this? I ask in my mind.
It's easier to not know or they're too scared to find
that spirit within us is where it all lies.
That essence of light, that soul in disguise,
just waiting for us to notice it's there,
for someone to love it and show that we care.
So back to myself and what I can give:
Well, it's just love and the proof that our departed still live.

No rules or timeouts

Not many people can honestly say
that they have never felt anger or pain.
It's one of those things that comes boxed with our life,
that we open again and again.

No matter how much we prepare
there is always an instance in life
where someone you love causes you hurt,
maybe your husband or wife.
There are no rules or timeouts.

Sometimes it's a constant fight,
sometimes we worry throughout the day
and it stops us from sleeping at night.
So how can we cope and how can we learn?

Is there a shortcut? we pray.
I'm afraid not, nope, this is your lot.
It will happen until your last day,
so I have to reveal its just how we deal,
it's just how we like to react.
So smile today, send your anger away
and your life will improve – that's a fact.

Are you a star in the sky?

Where are you? Are you a star in the sky?
You always told me that once you die, you die.
There is no heaven out there, there's nothing when you're gone.
You said that when a loved one dies, you just have to move on.

But I think I see a flaw in something that you said,
I simply can't believe your words
that when you're dead you're dead.
That sad day you left us, that day you closed your eyes,
was the hardest thing we ever did, saying our goodbyes.
The days that followed, pain and tears,
something that would last for years.

But even on that same night, I think I saw your spirit light.
I heard you sing your favourite song
and in it you said that you were wrong.
You told us heaven's really nice,
a beautiful place, a paradise.
You have met your family there,
the ones that gave you love and care.
You said that you're at peace right now
and wanted to tell us but didn't know how.
But now that you have found a way,
please come and visit every day.

A moment in time

As I look up at the starry sky,
I see you in the corner of my eye.
I shed a tear cos I wanted to touch,
please don't leave cos I'll miss you so much.

As night comes I'll sit and cry.
When I first heard, I wanted to die.
I still feel sad and that won't go;
you are so special and I love you so.

A moment in time was when I was born,
a moment I heard your very first scorn.
The moment you left me and went on your way,
these are moments I'll share for the rest of my day.

Trust us

When you look at your life and are feeling down,
you force a smile from a continual frown.
When your loved ones have passed and there's no-one to talk
and you've nothing to do but go for a walk.

You've given up hope, all that's left is despair
and you have nothing left from pulling out your hair.
Your kids have left home, have a life on their own,
you look at how quickly your children have grown.

Your mum and your dad are no longer here
and you have cried every last tear.
But why would this happen if God is around?
You're shouting for help, he hears not a sound.

Your spirit is dark, you're seeing no light.
Does life have to be a continual fight?
For happiness and love is all that you ask,
for a man that's so great it's not a big task.

If God's really listening, what would he say?
Have I been a bad person and now have to pay?
I'm closing my eyes just wanting to die.
I pray once again and ask my God: why?

I drift into sleep, for once I am calm,
in my own house I will come to no harm.
They say time's a healer, I'll wait and find out
and hurts in your heart that you have to let out.
I'll give it a try then to make happy this rhyme
and maybe it'll come just one day at a time.

Which star?

When we look at the stars what do we find?
The lights of our loved ones, or is that in our mind?
Heaven is somewhere, so where can it be?
I think it's in everyone, in you and in me.
The spirits that visit are loved ones we know,
the ones that we never wanted to go.
But how do they change, when they leave this great Earth?
It must be like dying and having a rebirth.

Those that had issues they couldn't get by
so that time would come when their body would die.
I look back to Christmas when I was a lad.
I never got many presents from my Dad.
But he did work hard for all that he got.
Christmas was special though there wasn't a lot.
So now we make sure that the kids have so much;
we like to give Christmas that family touch.
Not that we're rich, or have loads of dosh
and not cos were snobby, spoilt or posh.

It's just that this poem I don't want them to write,
I want them to have loved every day and night.
So to you lucky ones living out there,
just remember your folks do really care.
Think of the good times and how precious they are,
so you don't have to find them or wonder which star.

What happens when our loved ones die?

Tell me what happens when our loved ones die?
Are they really out there high up in the sky?
That place we call heaven is so far away,
I think of my loved ones every day.
Is it all final that physical death?
Or just a transition when they took their last breath?
I hope and I pray that they'll give me a sign,
one that assures me that they are still mine.

Sit quiet and listen and I'll tell you it all,
one to assure you and help you stand tall.
When we first die, you mourn for our loss
and let me tell you grieving is both of our boss.
For we miss that contact we had,
but only you think that dying is bad.
Once we have left that physical case,
our spirits move on to a much higher place.
Heaven you call but we call it home,
one thing's for sure, you are never alone.

Because we can visit in a blink of an eye
and our time in the spirit passes quickly by.
That's why sometimes in your world it seems long
before we drop by and sing you a song.
That song that you listen to that's sent to inspire,
to give you all hope and relight your fire.
I promise you, child, that I'm always there,

continued...

I blow on your cheek or I may touch your hair.
Those little things you dismiss all the time,
well that is just me, there to tell you I'm fine.

Our place in the spirit world has room for some more
and my hope is that one day you'll walk through my door.
Then I can show you this beautiful place
and restore your happiness on your beautiful face.
But until such time when your physical dies,
live your life happy, don't deal in lies.
Let yourself make a difference to the others around
and just keep on listening for my heavenly sound.

Spiritual truth

What is this spiritual truth we all ask?
Why is our life such a difficult task?
Why do we all have to argue and fight?
Why can't we sleep on it just for the night?
Things will be better when we all awake,
a deep calming breath is what we should take.

So now that we've taken one, let's see how we feel,
that one loving moment is what we should steal.
If we think that happiness comes to us free,
then we don't understand, or can we not see?
The life that we choose is not without trials,
we cannot avoid them, the frowns and the smiles.
The good and the bad times are what we shall face,
but sometimes we all need our own little space.

So now that we all understand how we live,
how much of our time are we willing to give?
To love your family, your neighbours and friends,
from the day you are born to the day your life ends.
But when your life ends it doesn't stop there,
we move to the spirit and that's when we share
the love of our family that passed on before –
they'll be ready to meet you as you come through that door.

That's when we've returned to that where we came
and realise that lessons were our primary aim.
The spiritual truth is what we shall see,
when we leave our physical and set ourselves free.

continued...

The journey we make to that new world of light
is like a bright new day after a long, dark night.
Then we have to look back on the things we have done,
through our physical life and to what we've become.
So why do we wait 'til we all leave our shell
to realise that were actually living in hell?
Let's live our lives to the best we can be
and share all our love to all that we see.
I don't mean go crazy and live like a nun,
but just be a good person and have lots of fun.

When you feel down

When you're feeling down and don't know why,
just look yourself right in the eye, tell yourself to try to smile,
then sit and ponder for a while.

There's 7 billion on this Earth,
all of them happy at their birth.
From then on they had their needs,
as Mother Nature sowed the seeds.

We all grow up and find our way,
that is why you're here today.
Look at what your troubles are
then just start to look afar.
Across the world at other lands,
see what food is in their hands.
For some there will be none at all;
they can't stand but most will fall.

So count your blessings on that fact
and think about how you can act.
Sometimes life is really tough
and you don't think you have enough.
But there's always someone there,
that also has a hope and a prayer.
They have no life, but don't complain,
about their suffering or their pain.

continued...

So think again, my dear friend,
when you want your life to end.
There is so much that you can do
to help yourself to make it through.
Think about them in that land,
then find a way to give a helping hand.

End of year

So the end of the year is upon us,
all that we've done is reflect.
Now we wonder what next year will bring for us
and what we can expect.
Another family member gone
or maybe two or three.
Will I lose somebody close,
or will they lose me?

We look at the good and the bad things,
and from everything we learn.
So we must make the most of life,
until it is our turn.
There's always so much we can do,
so much that we can find.
So look at what you have today
and happiness you will find.

Prestatyn

Here in Prestatyn outside the wind blows,
chilling and relaxing, hoping that it snows.
Just me and my wife away from the stress,
taking time off, no-one to impress.
Sitting here writing as the dark night falls,
listening to God's wind and hearing his calls.
Tonight is so special because we're alone,
no-one to talk to and no-one to phone.
So in comes the New Year, time for a new start,
relaxed and refreshed we will now play our part.
For this is the year where we step up a gear,
to bring happiness and joy, goodwill and good cheer.
The time for our spirit to find its goal,
then we can feel like we've nurtured our soul.

My life is good

My life is good at the moment.
I am happy in my work.
The choice I made three months ago,
I thought I'd go berserk.
Now when we look at what we need
and really think it through,
we find a path that's buried
in the minds of me and you.
It doesn't take much to take
a look at where you need to be,
just concentrate on your inner self –
it has all you need to see.

Missing you

It's not like I'll miss her now that she's passed,
I don't know how long that this grieving will last.
I was there every Friday at ten on the dot,
not once did I miss, I never forgot.
I'd tidy the house until it was clean,
then I'd cut her nails 'til her toes could be seen.
I still visit on Friday to clean for my dad,
but oh how I miss you and feeling so sad.

It's not been that long and I think of you lots.
I hear your sweet voice when I'm washing the pots.
I do have my moments and then phone my dad;
it makes me feel better when I'm feeling so sad.

Whenever I'm feeling you close to me now,
I wish I could touch you but I don't know how.
Then I go to sleep and I dream of you near;
I wake in the morning and it all becomes clear.

Minus one

What have I actually done in my sad and miserable life?
Have I brought happiness to my family, my kids and my wife?
Is it even worth it for my life to carry on?
Or would the world be better if it had a minus one?
People are dying every day. Are they the lucky souls?
Is dying their just reward for reaching all their goals?
There is no justice in the world. I'm always feeling sad.
It's just not fair I want to smile. I've never been that bad.

My family they all hate me now because of who I am.
In fact, the only one that cares is my sick and poorly mam.
So back to why I feel so low and why I want to die,
there's one good reason – that's my dad
    whose up there in the sky.
Maybe he could help me if I travelled to his home,
then I'd leave this sadness here and I wouldn't be alone.

So what is there to keep me here? There's nothing I confess.
So off I go to say hello to the spirit world I guess.

But then I look at life again and how the world is today,
and, all at once, my sad self pity seems to go away.
Cos what it is I'm seeing is there's always someone worse,
struggling with their humble life as if it is a curse.
But wait what's this – a news report of countries poor and sick.
I start reading all the facts – the poverty is thick.
There's families losing all their kids
    through sickness and poor diet,

continued...

whilst countries of the world look on and always keep their quiet.
A wave of guilt comes over me, anger at my self pity
feeling sorry for myself whilst the world is all so shitty.

So stand up straight – here is your goal, yes, this is what to do,
go outside a tell the world you're here because of you.
Let us see the sadness there and the help that we must give,
just a little time to spare to help these poor souls to live.
Take a look at your life – at least you have a door,
and know you always keep it closed to shield you from the poor.

I suppose that what I'm saying here is that
    we should count our blessings,
cos we can eat and drink nice things and heal with clean dressings.
That can't be said for all the countries on our planet that are poor,
so come on, stand for what is right, let's help them out some more.

Facebook friends

If you're still on my friends list from tonight,
then clearly you've done something right.
But if sadly you are not, then you're the ones I have forgot
and that is cos we never talk.
So goodbye friend and take a walk.

Living without fear

I wonder what it would be like to not have any fear,
not to worry about life or death and never shed a tear.
Not to be afraid of dark, spiders or a fight,
not to have a care of being a lonely soul at night.

If I had no more worries, life would be so good,
nothing ever makes you ill, not even the sight of blood.
How about an angry crowd or even to stand on stage,
none of that would bother me, not even my father's rage.

Yes, my life would be so great, without these fears I'm sure,
not to worry about money, greed or going out the door.
I could even walk the noisy streets at night,
without the worry of drunken revellers looking for a fight.

But life just isn't like that. Everyone's the same,
we all have challenges in our life, some kind of fear or pain.
It's learning how to deal with it that makes us even stronger,
some can cope so easily and for some it takes us longer.

A problem shared is a problem halved.
at least that's what they say,
so let's not keep it to ourselves - share it all today.

My dear friend Eve

I remember lots about my life, back when I was a kid,
so many special memories about the things that I did.
But that time comes and memories flood,
    for another soul we pray
and then we look back on our life, in a different sort of way.

Where do I start?
I ask myself, is this because I grieve?
Of course, it is. You see today I lost my dear friend Eve.
She said the letters that I wrote brought sunshine after rain.
I know she's in a better place, no longer in that pain.
She left her kids and husband Dave. He was always there,
especially when a daddy long legs was flying around my hair.

He would come and take it away because he knew my fear.
Life was so much better then, when Eve and Dave were near.
Dave, I'd like to say some words.
    I know some times were rough.
You've lost a lot of people you love, for you today is tough.
What good friends you have both been, all throughout my life,
I am so truly sorry that you have lost your loving wife.

Yes, she was a character and, of course, you'd hear her swear,
but that was her personality; we didn't really care.
As I grew and changed my life, time led us apart,
but let me tell you, Eve, my friend,
    you were always in my heart.
Friends don't have to see each other every single day;
it's the knowing that they're here for you - they never go away.

continued...

Well, Eve, now the time has come for you to leave this place.
I'll never hear that Cockney voice or see that smiley face.
I feel so sad but happy because I know you're near,
every time I think of you, I'll shed a little tear.
So go with love, my dear friend Eve, to that place up in the sky,
but visit me just once or twice to wipe my teary eye.

I needed to sleep

I needed to sleep I waited so long
and now you're listening to all those sad songs.
These songs are written for only one reason,
to get us through this sad passing season.
But as time goes by, the songs they will change
to happier ones in the partying range.
I never meant to leave you alone
but the time has to come when I have to go home.
I want to come back but that's not how it's done,
I'm missing my husband, my daughter and sons.

As I look around me at all I survey,
feeling that warmth of a nice sunny day.
I want for nothing because it's a spiritual thing,
I go to the mass and love when they sing.
The trees are green and the sky is blue,
I'm with all my family and that includes you.
I think of something and it is here,
I think of my family and I am near.
I can sit on my own and think of the past
and then I wonder how long this will last.

It lasts forever, says a voice that I know.
The love that you feel will never go.
I once saw a film that looked like this place,
I remember thinking now wouldn't that be ace.
Now I can see it in all its attire,
it feels very warm, but I don't need the fire.

I smell the flowers, I feel the grass,
I know there's no good time for a loved one to pass.
But we all have our time and I wait for you here,
I'll always be around cos I love you all so dear.

I may have left this painful life

I may have left this painful life
but I will forever be your wife.
I know we used to argue and fight,
you were my true guiding light.
The times when I laughed,
the times when I moan,
the times when I shouldn't have left you alone.

But remember the day that we first met
and all the good times we must never forget.
You may feel the hurt, you may feel the pain,
we never know how much time will remain.
To say all our words that we will never say
and then regret it on that really sad day.
But, hey, don't you cry and don't shed a tear
for things you will smile about after a year.

I know the times have been both bad and good,
but look what we made with mine and your blood.

We have four lovely kids and they have six more,
so we can't complain cos I've gone through that door.
Listen my love, for I must let you know:
of course, I moaned, but I did love you so.
We were together for so many years,
I now understand why you had all the fears.
I hope you remember the good and not bad
and those little away days that we always had.

continued...

The cheap and lovely Blackpool hotels,
my days in the bingo and the tempting food smells.
But know this, my love, although I'm not here,
just think of me and I will be near.
I'm sorry you're hurting and I say this out loud:
to know and to love you made me feel so proud.
I am happy here with my mum and dad
and I so hope these words will not make you sad.
Now I must go to set up my life,
in that new little cottage they've prepared for your wife.

How I became a Medium

When I saw you on that bed, I knew there was no hope.
I begged God not to let you die, I knew I wouldn't cope.
But God just didn't listen. That was the end of John
and so you left your loving kids. It's horrible now you're gone.
I cried so much and that's not me
    and thought my heart would break.
It did you know – I thought I'd had as much as I could take.
But one day something happened. I felt a little queer,
as I was walking up the stairs, I felt you drawing near.

I was a little scared and thought it was a ghost.
So I turned around, came back down and did myself some toast.
One Christmas Day I went to bed only for an hour
and when I woke I couldn't move, I felt this forceful power.
It wouldn't let me move or shout, I was frozen to the spot.
I prayed for help and shouted you, I thought I'd been forgot.
But then I was released and got up to tell my tale.
My wife knew there was something wrong cos I was looking pale.

I phoned my mam to tell her all the things about my fear,
I felt the love of you then Dad, you'd only gone this year.
I told her of the day you died and all the things she did.
Was I talking to my Dad? It's like I was a kid.
The excitement I was feeling was like when I was young,
it's like my dad was with my mam the second that I rung.
And just how was he telling me this? He couldn't, he was dead,
but wait a minute, I remember something that someone said.
The body may die but the spirit will live
    and always come with love

continued...

and this became the time when I believed in that heaven above.
So there my journey started, talking to the dead.
Every day I listened to these voices in my head.
Some would say I'm crazy, some would say I'm mad,
but I don't really care at all, because now I'm close to dad.

Having a brew

I've just been out to lock up the shed,
when I felt the urge to lift up my head.
What I could see was a cluster of stars
and what I could hear was the noise of the cars.
Just how quiet would it be in the sky
to sit with the stars and watch time go by?
The peace you would feel I can't comprehend,
I'm sure the world's problems I could definitely mend.
But it just isn't real and I can't touch the sky,
but all the world's problems, I think I could try.
Just by being nice and send out a prayer,
and loving my neighbour even when I'm not there.
There's lots of things I think we could do,
like visiting loved ones and having a brew.
The smallest of steps can get us about
and if everyone took that time to go out,
to look at the world and see what we have,
to heal it and share and fill it with love.
So don't sit here reading about what we could do.
Put on the kettle and then make a brew,
invite your neighbour and show them you care
and help out this world to make it more fair.

Carry me in your heart

Carry me in your heart, don't ever let me go,
even when you're feeling down, say you love me so.
Be my friend, be my guide in everything you do,
to thine own self and to me, your heart it must be true.
For I am your conscience and I am here, whatever is in your life.
I am here when all is lost I am your husband, your children,
your parents, your wife.

Let not be lost that which you hold dear,
nor let it be tainted or soured.
Let all about you be blessed and true
and the life that you live be empowered.

Are all of your needs actually just that,
or are they the wants of your soul?
Just take out the bad and work with the good,
that will help to reach your goal.
And just as I said right until you are dead
and maybe a bit after that,
I will be there when you're pulling your hair,
knowing you've just kicked the cat.
So fear me ye not for I am your friend,
but sometimes I'm also your foe.
But rely on me now and anytime soon,
for I love you and I'll never go.

A tough audience

As I stand there on the stage,
the audience all cross armed.
How can I get through to them?
I'm feeling quite alarmed.
I have their family with me here,
bringing all their love.
Their mums their dads and all their friends,
those in heaven above.

Sitting there not listening
to what I've got to say.
They must want a message now
or why else would they pay.
So off I go to start my show,
a Medium is what I do.

First messages great, then there's a wait,
because no-one takes the next two.
From then on the task was set
to get them relaxed and calm.
And help them all to understand
that it's love they'll get not harm.

Once I'd finished I sat down,
with my lovely cup of tea.
I can't believe it was at that time
that they come over to me.
I could take all that you said
and I'm feeling really bad.
For that man you described so
brilliantly was actually my dad.

continued...

Why didn't you say, I said surprised,
if the evidence was that good.
Well, she said I hated him,
even though he's my flesh and blood.
And so it makes me wonder,
I will until my dying day:
why do they come to see a Medium
and also have to pay
just to sit there, not take part
in the greatest thing we've had
and just ignore the Medium
when he brings her doting dad?
It's not for me to answer
because that is not my job,
so when this happens all again,
I'll just smile and shut my gob.

A mother's love

I may not be a handsome prince, a king or even queen,
I may not even be a person you have ever seen.
I may not be the person you would give the time of day,
I may even be the person you would tell to go away.

For I may leave this Earth one day not done a single thing,
I may even leave this place and never learned to sing.
I may not have a wife or kids, my own home or a job,
I may not figure in your heart for you to even sob.
But when I'm born I have one thing sent from God above,
the most valued and most precious thing,
yes, that's my mother's love.

A holiday break

Sitting alone in a foreign place,
looking at the sunshine, a smile on my face.
Nothing to worry, nothing to care,
back home is so far away, in my mind, it's not there.

We all need a holiday at some time in our life,
a chance to get away from the trouble and strife.
It doesn't have to cost much, nor worry about fat –
there's the rest of your life to worry about that.
Sitting alone planning my day,
shall I keep busy or just witter it away.

It doesn't really matter, I don't really care,
there's nothing to worry me or get in my hair.
So now I shall sign off and go have a beer,
maybe some water or tasty sangria.
Spend some quality time with my wife
and make some great plans for the rest of our life.

You are strange

Who do you think you are, doing well for yourself?
All your dreams and hope should be getting dusty on the shelf.
Who do you think you are, thinking you can do some good?
You'll always be a failure, it says so in your blood.
What do you think you're doing, talking to the dead?
I think that there is something wrong, a problem with your head.
Face the harsh reality, your life has been foretold,
don't even try to change it, don't go getting bold.

Now just listen here, my friend, let me tell you how I tick:
it is my life, I'll live it well, so feel free to take the Mick.
I can't sit here and just do nowt, I had to change my life.
I realised that if I don't change, I'll lose my kids and wife.
But what do you think happened, when I let it start to change?
I find that I have different views and don't find people strange.
I actually now enjoy myself and loving what I do,
I don't get drunk – well, not all the time –
it's just as nice to have a brew.

A cup of tea, that's all it takes, a sit down and a chat,
not about the negative stuff – I've seen the end of that.
Now, my friend, you have your life, and a choice to make it good,
don't get bogged down in that belief, that it's all in your blood.
You have a right to make your mark upon the world we live
and not to take from everyone; we can also give.
Take a look around you and see what you would like,
to make that smile a real one and tell your stress to take a hike.

continued...

All you have to do is want it, it's there for you for free.
Happiness is for everyone, especially me and you.
I'm not trying to persuade. I'm just telling you what is true,
I'm not even trying to explain myself or trying to make you see.
What I have is what I want, it's taken a lot of graft,
so you can please yourself, my friend, and you can think I'm daft.
I have no reason nor no doubt that you are wanting change,
so do it and be happy now, then you won't find me so strange.

What a life

Wake in the morning feeling down,
have a quick wash and it's off to the town.
Look for a job but what's the point.
I think I'll roll myself a joint.
Pick up my dole cheque at half-past two,
buy a few cans of special brew.

Meet the lads on the seats in the square,
get out the weed we can all have a share.
Here comes the rain, needing some shelter,
get ourselves arrested – the cells are a belter.
Free cup of tea and even a meal.
I am in heaven or that's how I feel.

Bed for the night, a room of my own,
but I'm sobering up now and want to go home.
But there lies the problem that only I know,
I have nowhere to live and nowhere to go.
So I'll just get my head down and sleep for the night,
things may be different in the cold morning light.

Wake up again and still feeling down,
getting released and go back to town.
Light up a joint. It's just half-past ten
and so begins my life's cycle again.

This is the life

Wake in the morning go for run,
a swim and jacuzzi, then a nice toasted bun.
Go to the office, which is, of course, very posh,
sign some papers then a game of squash.
Browse the internet for a nice break,
which of my Bentleys deciding to take.
Or maybe I'll leave them to get them all waxed,
by my live-in chauffer who I've hired for the tax.

So what shall I do for the rest of the day?
I'm getting quite bored so need to play.
Another board meeting, beginning to yawn,
sometimes wishing I'd never been born.
Oh hang on a minute, I know what I'll do,
I'll book a penthouse in the Hilton Peru.
That should do it and put a smile on my face,
now for the meeting I'd best show my face.

Bored again as he talks so much crap,
just get on with it now there's a nice chap.
All I can think of is where can I go,
I don't have to be here – I am the CEO.
Make my excuses and get up and leave,
I couldn't care less if they don't believe.
For now I'm away I mustn't forget,
I don't need my Bentleys – I'll go on my private jet.

You're on holiday

I'm not being funny and I don't like to boast,
but I'm sitting down while the missus makes toast.
The father-in-law is here I can see,
so I asked very nicely for him to make tea.

Down to the beach for a bathe and a swim,
maybe an hour in the hotel's posh gym.
This is the life that I wanted, I say;
it won't last long though cos were on holiday.

Another few days to get a nice tan,
but first we'll get some nice grub in the pan.
Then down to the bar for a drink cos were hot;
it's such a great place when you're here in S'illot.

Go down to Arta to see an old friend,
take a wrong turn and went round a bend.
The sat nav once more for the price that it cost,
took a good shouting cos it got us lost.
It doesn't really matter, it's not such a pain,
because wherever you end up, you're in beautiful Spain.

More Facebook

Looking at Facebook, it's probably wrong,
seeing the status and the odd crappy song.
Been to the toilet, making a brew,
having a clear out, they might unfriend you.
Here's someone arguing, threatening a life,
telling that someone has slept with their wife.

Refresh the page, look down again,
getting a friend request from someone called Ben.
Look at his profile, see if he's all right,
don't want another friend wanting to fight.
Make sure my comments are all PC,
don't want the haters picking on me.

I'm getting quite tired with all of these rules,
maybe I'll open some Facebook schools.
But just for now, I will bid you good day,
I have a life and I'll live it today.
Hang on what's that, someone's sent a PM,
that means private message.

It's from my new friend Ben.
What is he saying? I must take a peek
and I'll probably unfriend him after this week.
I take a quick look. He just wants to say hi.
I say hello back and then bid him goodbye.
I'm going for dinner and then feed the cat
and I'll come back on later for a nice little chat.

A heart of stone

You used to be so hard on me and never understood.
I would try to make you see that I was really good.
You would always pass me by, to give praise to another,
I bent over backwards to help you to discover.
The heart I had was large and big enough for two,
but also big enough to break and that was done by you.
I wasn't strong enough inside and couldn't make you see
that you had my heart strings, had a choice to set them free.
I guess your heart was made of stone and was just too cold to melt,
so you couldn't see the hurt inside, the hurt that I had felt.
As I grew I'm sure you knew our paths would lead apart,
a brand new home, a wife to share, one I could give my heart.
I guess I must have tried too hard, as I sit here and take stock,
for that one too was just like you and also made of rock.

From then on I hid myself away from hurt and pain,
it's all that I can do right now to stop going insane.
Maybe one day my time will come and from this world I'll part
and I will find what's deep inside and that's your loving heart.
But last night in my dreams I saw your big blue eyes.
You said you came to show me love and to apologise.
I tried to hold back the tears because I never knew
that you always loved me so and last night you were true.
You said you were so sad you'd gone, that God had made us part,
but you just came back to show that love was in your heart.

Now that time has come for me to travel to my home,
no more sadness from this earth, no empty plains to roam.
There's just one thing that makes me cry but not because I'm sad,
standing there to greet me is my big hearted blue-eyed dad.

continued...

As humans, we have dramas the ones like on TV.
We try to tell ourselves the only perfect one is me.
But let me tell you now, my friend, you're just like all the rest,
sometimes you can be an annoying and sometimes you're the best.
We like to think we're perfect, we think it's in our blood,
we like to think that we are angels working for the good.
We like to tell our audience that we do it all for you,
but deep down in our broken hearts we know that isn't true.
We all have problems at some time, it's really part of life.
We soon grow up then find work and find a husband or a wife.
Tragedies are there in life, we lose someone we love,
that tired body just gives up and goes to heaven above.
Of course, we're sad and mortified because they have to leave
and for a year or maybe two we take our time to grieve.

Now here's a fact I'll tell you, I hope you see it's true:
there's not one bit of difference between me and you.
Cut us and we'll bleed you know, we're happy and we're blue.
Neither of us is perfect and that's an actual fact,
so on that note, let's sit down and we can make a pact.
To not let life defeat us, or let it make us sad,
let's understand that life will bring us good and bad.
It's living through this trial here that makes us all so strong.
Only when you've loved and lost can you sing your own song.

But just remember, as I said at the beginning of this rhyme:
you're not perfect and all the hurts will heal themselves in time.
Just believe that you are you, with all your faults and trials,
so go through life without a care and fill it full of smiles.

A little bit of sunshine

A little bit of sunshine seems to put things right,
a bright and shiny brand new day after a long and dreary night.
Tossing and turning worries on my mind,
the answers to dilemmas that I can never find.
But now it all seems crystal – there's happiness inside,
I have a smile across my face and my heart is filled with pride.
The reason for this change of heart whilst looking at the sun
Is, of course, because it's bright and a new day has begun.
Life isn't always perfect and we'll never get it right
and sometimes all your thoughts mix up
  when you try to sleep at night.

There's nothing we can do sometimes, it's just a fact of life,
to worry about the things you care for,
  the things that give you strife.
So if you want perspective to measure all your woes,
look across the ocean where there's countries with no clothes.
Nothing in their pantries, diseased and full of pain,
measure all your worries and then measure them again.
They'll pale into insignificance, or at least I hope they do
and if they don't, I'm sorry because the ones I talk of must be you.

Time to go

What's it like in heaven God, is there a place for me?
Will I have to earn my stripes?
Please just let me see.
I know I've not done my best in life, I know that I've been bad,
I have taken other lives and made so many sad.
But now this body is growing old and has the dreaded C,
I don't think it will be long, the doctor said to me.

So as I pray to you today and ask you for a place,
tell me you have plans for me once you see my face.
Will I dance or get the chance to look back on my deeds?
Can I make it right for those I've hurt? Can I sow new seeds?
All I've ever wanted was to earn respect,
but maybe it was fear I gained now that I reflect.

There's nothing I can say or do to change the things I've done,
repentance is the only way and now that has begun.
Don't get me wrong, as I sing this song I'm not afraid of death,
I just want peace at last once I have drawn my last breath.
So please forgive and let me through those heavenly pearly gates,
so I can have light shoulders and remove these heavy weights.

End of a holiday

Today's the day. It's been a blast. I have to say it's gone so fast,
drinking beer has helped I think.
    I breath out hard and what a stink.
Under my arms I smell a lot,
    there's food left over beginning to rot.

So as I look upon my tan, I think I've done the best I can.
My head is fuzzy, legs like jelly, I also have a podgy belly.
So tomorrow it's off to the gym, work out hard to get me slim.
That idea I start to snub, because here is Karen with my grub,
sausages, bacon just for me, all swilled down with a mug of tea.

Looking outside on my last day, the sun is shining,
    I'm feeling gay.
Of course, I mean happy with a smile on my face
because I've enjoyed myself in this place,
so off I go to eat my food,
    then one last chance to sunbathe nude.
As I look around I best leave soon,
because the whalers are coming with their harpoon.
Only kidding, I'm not like a whale,
but I am getting thirsty and I've run out of ale.
So it's off to the German bar for one last beer,
then it's adios amigo, cos I'm getting out of here.